barefoot ragamuffin curricula

www.barefootmeandering.com

veritas • gnaritas • libertas

Blossoming Workbook

Manuscript

English Lessons Through Literature

Clouds
by Christina G. Rossetti

White sheep, white sheep,
On a blue hill,
When the wind stops
You all stand still;

When the wind blows
You walk away slow,
White sheep, white sheep,
Where do you go?

Suddenly Uncle Henry stood up.

"There's a cyclone coming, Em," he called to his wife.

"There's a cyclone coming, Em," he called to his wife.

White sheep, white sheep,

On a blue hill,

When the wind stops

You all stand still;

"Who is Aunt Em?" inquired

the little old woman.

"She is my aunt who lives in

Kansas, where I came from."

"Who is Aunt Em?" inquired

the little old woman.

If at first you don't succeed,

try, try again.

"Come along, Toto," she

said. "We will go to the

Emerald City and ask the

Great Oz how to get

back to Kansas again."

"We will go to the Emerald City

and ask the Great Oz how to

get back to Kansas again."

So she told him all about

Kansas, and how gray

everything was there, and how

the cyclone had carried her

to this queer Land of Oz.

So she told him all about Kansas

and how the cyclone had carried

her to this queer Land of Oz.

Clouds

When the wind blows

You walk away slow,

White sheep, white sheep,

Where do you go?

The Tin Woodman gave a sigh

of satisfaction and lowered his

axe, which

he leaned against the tree.

The Tin Woodman gave a sigh of

satisfaction and lowered his axe,

which he leaned against the tree.

A bird in the hand is worth

two in the bush.

Narration: The Young Crab and His Mother

Narration: The Young Crab and His Mother

The Months
by Sara Coleridge, adapted by Kathy Jo DeVore

January brings the snow,
Makes our feet and fingers glow.

February brings the rain,
Thaws the frozen lake again.

March brings breezes loud and shrill,
Stirs the dancing daffodil.

April brings the primrose sweet,
Scatters daisies at our feet.

May brings flocks of pretty lambs,
Skipping by their fleecy dams.

June brings tulips, lilies, roses,
Fills the children's hand with posies.

Hot July brings cooling showers,
Apricots and gilliflowers.

August brings the sheaves of corn,
Then the harvest home is borne.

Warm September brings the fruit,
Sportsmen then begin to shoot.

Fresh October brings the pheasants,
Then to gather nuts is pleasant.

Dull November brings the blast,
Then the leaves are whirling fast.

Chill December brings the sleet,
Blazing fire, and Christmas treat.

The Tin Woodman chopped

a great pile of wood with

his axe, and Dorothy built a

splendid fire that warmed her

and made her feel less lonely.

The Wonderful Wizard of Oz, Chapter 7

Dorothy built a splendid fire

that warmed her and made

her feel less lonely.

January brings the snow,

Makes our feet and fingers glow.

February brings the rain,

Thaws the frozen lake again.

It was a lovely country,

with plenty of flowers and

fruit trees and sunshine to

cheer them, and had they

not felt so sorry for the

poor Scarecrow, they could

have been very happy.

It was a lovely country, with

plenty of flowers and fruit trees

and sunshine to cheer them.

Fools rush in where angels

fear to tread.

"We cannot be far from the road of yellow brick, now," remarked the Scarecrow as he stood beside the girl, "for we have come nearly as far as the river carried us away."

The Wonderful Wizard of Oz, Chapter 9

"We cannot be far from the

road of yellow brick, now,"

remarked the Scarecrow.

It was some time before the

Cowardly Lion awakened,

for he had lain among the

poppies a long while, breathing

in their deadly fragrance.

March brings breezes loud

and shrill,

Stirs the dancing daffodil.

April brings the primrose sweet,

Scatters daisies at our feet.

"But I spoke to him as he sat behind his screen and gave him your message. He said he will grant you an audience, if you so desire."

The Wonderful Wizard of Oz, Chapter 11

"But I spoke to him as he

sat behind his screen and

gave him your message."

A man is known by the

company he keeps.

Narration: The Boy and the Filberts

So they called the yellow

Winkies and asked them if

they would help to rescue their

friends, and the Winkies said

that they would be delighted

to do all in their power

for Dorothy, who had set

them free from bondage.

May brings flocks of pretty lambs,

Skipping by their fleecy dams.

June brings tulips, lilies, roses,

Fills the children's hand with posies.

"Suppose we call the field mice," she suggested. "They could probably tell us the way to the Emerald City."

The Wonderful Wizard of Oz, Chapter 14

"Suppose we call the field

mice," she suggested "They

could probably tell us the way

to the Emerald City."

Keep your nose to the grindstone.

"Then I thought, as the country was so green and beautiful, I would call it the Emerald City."

The Wonderful Wizard of Oz, Chapter 15

"Then I thought, as the country

was so green and beautiful, I would

call it the Emerald City."

Then he said goodbye to them

all in a cheerful voice and went

to the Throne Room, where

he rapped upon the door.

The Wonderful Wizard of Oz, Chapter 16

Then he said goodbye to them

all in a cheerful voice and went

to the Throne Room.

The Months

Hot July brings cooling showers,

Apricots and gilliflowers.

August brings the sheaves of corn,

Then the harvest home is borne.

"Thank you," he answered.

"Now, if you will help me sew

the silk together, we will begin

to work on our balloon."

The Wonderful Wizard of Oz, Chapter 17

"Now, if you will help me sew

the silk together, we will begin

to work on our balloon."

All good things must

come to an end.

Narration: The Crow and the Pitcher

Narration: The Crow and the Pitcher

As Dorothy bade the good-natured Guardian a last farewell, she said, "I have been very kindly treated in your lovely City, and everyone has been good to me. I cannot tell you how grateful I am."

The Wonderful Wizard of Oz, Chapter 19

"I have been very kindly treated

in your lovely City, and everyone

has been good to me."

Warm September brings fruit to eat,

Apples and melons and berries

so sweet.

Fresh October brings the pheasants,

Then to gather nuts is pleasant.

So the Scarecrow climbed

farther up and sat down

on the top of the wall, and

Dorothy put her head over

and cried, "Oh, my!" just as

the Scarecrow had done.

Jan.

Feb.

Mar.

Apr.

May

Jun.

Jul.

Aug.

Sep.

Oct.

Nov.

Dec.

Knowledge is power.

"Not a bit of it," answered the Lion. "I should like to live here all my life. See how soft the dried leaves are under your feet and how rich and green the moss is that clings to these old trees."

The Wonderful Wizard of Oz, Chapter 21

"Not a bit of it," answered

the Lion. "I should like to

live here all my life."

"Who are you?" asked the Scarecrow.

Then a head showed itself over the rock, and the same voice said, "This hill belongs to us, and we don't allow anyone to cross it."

The Wonderful Wizard of Oz, Chapter 22

"This hill belongs to us, and we don't allow anyone to cross it."

Dull November brings the blast,

Then the leaves are whirling fast.

Chill December brings the sleet,

Blazing fire, and Christmas treat.

"Why have you come to the South Country?"

"To see the Good Witch who rules here," she answered.

"Will you take me to her?"

"To see the Good Witch who

rules here," she answered.

"Will you take me to her?"

to   too   two

witch   which

here   hear

Better safe than sorry.

Narration: The Kid and the Wolf

Four Seasons of the Year
adapted by Kathy Jo DeVore

On March the twenty-first is spring,
When little birds begin to sing;
Begin to build and hatch their brood,
And carefully provide them food.

Summer's the twenty-first of June,
The cuckoo changes then his tune;
All nature smiles, the fields look gay,
The weather's fair to make the hay.

September, on the twenty-third,
Migration begins for many a bird;
Autumn comes in; the fields are shorn,
The fruits are ripe; so is the corn.

Winter's cold frosts and northern blasts,
The season is we mention last;
The date of which in truth we must
Fix for December: twenty-first.

"Where are you going to, dear bear?" asked Snow-white.

"I must go to the wood and protect my treasure from the wicked dwarfs. In winter, when the earth is frozen hard, they are obliged to remain underground."

The Blue Fairy Book: *Snow-white and Rose-red*

"In winter, when the earth is

frozen hard, they are obliged

to remain underground."

On March the twenty-first

is spring,

When little birds begin to sing,

Begin to build and hatch their brood,

And carefully provide them food.

"Very well then," said the

North Wind. "But you must

sleep here tonight, for if we

are ever to get there, we

must have the day before us."

"But you must sleep here tonight,

for if we are ever to get there we

must have the day before us."

Many kinfolk, few friends.

Then he went down into the garden, and though it was winter everywhere else, here the sun shone, and the birds sang, and the flowers bloomed, and the air was soft and sweet.

The Blue Fairy Book: *Beauty and the Beast*

Here the sun shone, and the birds

sang, and the flowers bloomed, and

the air was soft and sweet.

The poor child, who did not know it was dangerous to stay and hear a wolf talk, said to him, "I am going to see my grandmama and carry her a custard and a little pot of butter from my mama."

Summer's the twenty-first of June,

The cuckoo changes then his tune;

All nature smiles, the fields look gay.

The weather's fair to make the hay.

Then the Queen began to

cry and sob so bitterly

that the little man was

sorry for her and said, "I

will give you three days to

guess my name, and if you

find it out in that time,

you may keep your child."

The Blue Fairy Book: *Rumpelstiltzkin*

"I'll give you three days to guess my

name, and if you find it out in that

time, you may keep your child."

Don't bite the hand that feeds you.

Narration: The Boy Bathing

The children had not been

able to sleep for hunger

and had heard what their

step-mother had said to

their father. Grettel wept

bitterly and said to Hansel,

"Now it's all up with us."

The Blue Fairy Book: Hansel and Grettel

The moon was shining clearly,

and the white pebbles which

lay in front of the house

glittered like bits of silver.

September, on the twenty-third,

Migration begins for many a bird;

Autumn comes in; the fields are shorn,

The fruits are ripe; so is the corn.

"You saved my life in the meadow by the willow tree, and I promised that I would repay you. Take this. It is Princess Goldilocks's ring."

Mighty oaks from little

acorns grow.

"What good would it do him

to be rich, or handsome, or

to possess all the kingdoms of

the world if he were wicked?

You know he would still be

unhappy. Only a good man

can be really contented."

"You know he would still be
unhappy. Only a good man
can be really contented."

He then blew such a tantivy

that the giant awoke and

came out of his den, crying

out, "You saucy villain! You

shall pay for this. I'll broil

you for my breakfast!"

The Blue Fairy Book: *The History of Jack the Giant-Killer*

I am   we are   you are

he is   she is   it is

they are   I will   we will

he will   she will   they will

Winter's cold frosts and northern

blasts,

The season is we mention last;

The date of which in truth we must

Fix for December: twenty—first.

Then Ali Baba climbed

down and went to the door

concealed among the bushes

and said, "Open, Sesame!"

The Blue Fairy Book: *The Forty Thieves*

Then Ali Baba climbed

down and went to the door

concealed among the bushes

and said, "Open, Sesame!"

Better be alone than in bad company.

Narration: The Boys and the Frogs

Monday's Child
A Mother Goose Rhyme,
adapted by Kathy Jo DeVore

Monday's child is fair of face,
Tuesday's child is full of grace,

Wednesday's child is full of delight,
Thursday's child is happy and bright,

Friday's child is loving and kind,
Saturday's child has a good mind,

And the child that is born on Sunday
Is happy and sunny and loves to play.

"You see how self—love keeps

us from knowing our own

defects of mind and body."

"You see how self—love keeps

us from knowing our own

defects of mind and body."

Sun.

Mon.

Tue.

Wed.

Thu.

Fri.

Sat.

Monday's child is fair of face,

Tuesday's child is full of grace,

Mrs. Darling first heard of
Peter when she was tidying
up her children's minds. It is
the nightly custom of every
good mother after her children
are asleep to rummage in
their minds and put things
straight for next morning.

Peter Pan, Chapter 1

Mrs. Darling first heard of

Peter when she was tidying

up her children's minds.

Money doesn't grow on trees.

"Nana, it isn't six o'clock yet. Oh dear, oh dear, I shan't love you any more, Nana. I tell you I won't be bathed. I won't. I won't!"

Peter Pan, Chapter 2

is not   are not   was not

were not   do not   does not

did not   have not   has not

had not   could not   will not

He had to translate. "She
is not very polite. She says
you are a great ugly girl and
that she is my fairy."

"She is not very polite. She

says you are a great ugly girl

and that she is my fairy."

Wednesday's child is full of delight,

Thursday's child is happy and bright,

Friday's child is loving and kind,

Saturday's child has a good mind,

"That is the awful thing, John.
We should have to go on, for
we don't know how
to stop."

This was true. Peter
had forgotten to show
them how to stop.

Peter Pan, Chapter 4

"That is the awful thing, John.

We should have to go on, for

we don't know how to stop."

Absence makes the heart grow fonder.

Narration: The Fox and the Grapes

Narration: The Fox and the Grapes

In a tremble they opened the
street door. Mr. Darling would
have rushed upstairs, but Mrs.
Darling signed him to go softly.

Peter Pan, Chapter 3

Mr. Darling would have rushed

upstairs, but Mrs. Darling

signed him to go softly.

And the child that is born on Sunday

Is happy and sunny and loves to play.

When she sat down to a

basketful of their stockings,

every heel with a hole in it,

she would fling up her arms

and exclaim, "Oh dear, I

am sure I sometimes think

spinsters are to be envied!"

Peter Pan, Chapter 7

Good fences make good neighbors.

He sighs   said Smee.

He sighs again   said

Starkey.

And yet a third time he

sighs   said Smee.

"We are on the rock, Wendy," he

said. "But it is growing smaller.

Soon the water will be over it."

What Is Pink?
By Christina G. Rossetti

What is pink? A rose is pink
By the fountain's brink.

What is red? A poppy's red
In its barley bed.

What is blue? The sky is blue
Where the clouds float through.

What is white? A swan is white
Sailing in the light.

What is yellow? Pears are yellow,
Rich and ripe and mellow.

What is green? The grass is green,
With small flowers between.

What is violet? Clouds are violet
In the summer twilight.

What is orange? Why, an orange,
Just an orange!

Well, not only could they not

understand each other, but

they forgot their manners.

Peter Pan, Chapter 9

Well, not only could they not

understand each other, but

they forgot their manners.

What is pink? A rose is pink

By the fountain's brink.

What is red? A poppy's red

In its barley bed.

"Oh yes, Tinker Bell will tell you," Wendy retorted scornfully. "She is an abandoned little creature."

Peter Pan, Chapter 10

"Oh yes, Tinker Bell will tell you,"

Wendy retorted scornfully. "She

is an abandoned little creature."

A watched pot never boils.

_____

_____

_____

_____

Narration: The Farmer and His Sons

Every foot of ground between

the spot where Hook had

landed his forces and the

home under the trees was

stealthily examined.

Peter Pan, Chapter 12

Every foot of ground between the

spot where Hook had landed his

forces and the home under the

trees was stealthily examined.

What is blue? The sky is blue

Where the clouds float through.

What is white? A swan is white

Sailing in the light.

Do you believe   he cried.

What do you think she asked Peter.

Peter Pan, Chapter 13

Lesson 50 Exercise

She was saying that she thought

she could get well again if

children believed in fairies.

Good things come to those who wait.

She was wrapped in the

blanket of night, through

which no sound from her could

have reached the shore.

Peter Pan, Chapter 14

She was wrapped in the

blanket of night, through

which no sound from her could

have reached the shore.

What is yellow? Pears are yellow,

Rich and ripe and mellow.

What is green? The grass is green,

With small flowers between.

"John," he said, looking around

him doubtfully.

"I think I have been

here before."

Peter Pan, Chapter 16

"John," he said, looking around

him doubtfully, "I think I

have been here before."

Where there is a will there is a way.

Narration: The Ants and the Grasshopper

It was too late. The boat

struck the bank full tilt.

The dreamer, the joyous

oarsman, lay on his back

at the bottom of the boat,

his heels in the air.

The dreamer, the joyous

oarsman, lay on his back at

the bottom of the boat,

his heels in the air.

What Is Pink?

What is violet? Clouds are violet

In the summer twilight.

What Is Pink?

What is orange? Why, an orange,

Just an orange!

Slushy green undergrowth

Where the roach swim—

Here we keep our larder,

Cool and full and dim.

The Wind in the Willows, Chapter 2

Slushy green undergrowth

Where the roach swim—

Here we keep our larder,

Cool and full and dim.

Neither a borrower nor a lender be.

"Can we eat a doormat? Can

we sleep under a doormat?

Can we sit on a doormat and

sledge home over the snow on

it, you exasperating rodent?"

The Wind in the Willows, Chapter 3

"Can we sit on a doormat and
sledge home over the snow on
it, you exasperating rodent?"

All But Blind
By Walter de la Mare

All but blind
In his cambered hole
Gropes for worms
The four-clawed Mole.

All but blind
In the evening sky
The hooded Bat
Twirls softly by.

All but blind
In the burning day
The Barn-Owl blunders
On her way.

And blind as are
These three to me,
So blind to someone
I must be.

"How on earth, Badger," he said at last, "did you ever find time and strength to do all this? It's astonishing!"

"How on earth, Badger," he

said at last, "did you ever find

time and strength to do all

this? It's astonishing!"

All but blind

In his cambered hole

Gropes for worms

The four—clawed Mole.

"What is it, old fellow?

Whatever can be the matter?

Tell us your trouble, and let

me see what I can do."

"What is it, old fellow? Whatever can

be the matter? Tell us your trouble,

and let me see what I can do."

A fool and his money are soon parted.

_____

_____

_____

_____

Narration: The Wolf and the Crane

Narration: The Wolf and the Crane

All but blind

In the evening sky

The hooded Bat

Twirls softly by.

"You are a good, kind, clever girl," he said, "and I am indeed a proud and a stupid toad. Introduce me to your worthy aunt, if you will be so kind."

The Wind in the Willows, Chapter 8

"You are a good, kind, clever girl," he said, "and I am indeed a proud and a stupid toad. Introduce me to your worthy aunt, if you will be so kind."

Never judge a book by its cover.

Addresses:

Mr. Mole
3264 River Edge
River Bank 40324

Mr. Water Rat
3264 River Edge
River Bank 40324

Mr. Badger
8525 Badger Den
The Wild Wood 40426

Mr. Toad
6342 Stout Castle
Remote Dungeon 50367

"Why, where are you off to,
Ratty?" asked the Mole.

"Going South, with the rest
of them," murmured the
Rat in a dreamy monotone.

"Seawards first and then
on shipboard, and so to the
shores that are calling me!"

"Going South, with the rest of them," murmured the Rat in a dreamy monotone. "Seawards first and then on shipboard, and so to the shores that are calling me!"

Toad's temper, which had

been simmering viciously

for some time, now fairly

boiled over, and he lost

all control of himself.

The Wind in the Willows, Chapter 10

Lesson 64 Exercise

Toad's temper, which had been

simmering viciously for some

time, now fairly boiled over, and

he lost all control of himself.

All but blind

In the burning day

The Barn-Owl blunders

On her way.

"Toad!" he said severely.

"You bad, troublesome little

animal! Aren't you ashamed

of yourself? What do you

think your father, my old

friend, would have said?"

The Wind in the Willows, Chapter 10

"Toad!" he said severely. "You bad,

troublesome little animal! Aren't

you ashamed of yourself?"

Beauty is only skin deep.

Narration: The Hare and the Tortoise

It had, in fact, a sort of mixed

flavor of cherry tart, custard,

pineapple, roast turkey, toffy,

and hot buttered toast.

It had, in fact, a sort of mixed

flavor of cherry tart, custard,

pineapple, roast turkey, toffy,

and hot buttered toast.

And blind as are

These three to me,

So blind to someone

I must be.

Commas in a Series

Alice took up the fan and

gloves, and, as the hall

was very hot, she kept

fanning herself all the time

she went on talking.

Alice's Adventures in Wonderland, Chapter 2

"Curiouser and curiouser!" cried

Alice (she was so much surprised

that, for the moment, she quite

forgot how to speak good English).

Don't count your chickens

before they hatch.

"Mine is a long and a sad tale!"

said the Mouse, turning to

Alice and sighing.

"It is a long tail, certainly,"

said Alice, looking down with

wonder at the Mouse's tail,

"but why do you call it sad?"

"It is a long tail, certainly,"

said Alice, looking down with

wonder at the Mouse's tail,

"but why do you call it sad?"

The Rainbow
By Christina G. Rossetti

Boats sail on the rivers,
And ships sail on the seas;
But clouds that sail across the sky
Are prettier than these.

There are bridges on the rivers,
As pretty as you please;
But the bow that bridges heaven,
And overtops the trees,
And builds a road from earth to sky,
Is prettier far than these.

"Don't be particular. Here, Bill! Catch hold of this rope. Will the roof bear? Mind that loose slate. Oh, it's coming down! Heads below!"

Alice's Adventures in Wonderland, Chapter 4

"Don't be particular. Here, Bill!

Catch hold of this rope. Will the

roof bear? Mind that loose slate.

Oh, it's coming down! Heads below!"

The Rainbow

Boats sail on the rivers,

And ships sail on the seas;

But clouds that sail across the sky

Are prettier than these.

Alice thought she might as

well wait, as she had nothing

else to do, and perhaps

after all it might tell her

something worth hearing.

Alice's Adventures in Wonderland, Chapter 5

Alice thought she might as well

wait, as she had nothing else to

do, and perhaps after all it might

tell her something worth hearing.

Beggars can't be choosers.

Review: Nouns, Pronouns, Verbs, Adjectives

Narration: Hercules and the Wagoner

A Dormouse was sitting between them, fast asleep, and the other two were using it as a cushion, resting their elbows on it, and talking over its head.

A Dormouse was sitting between

them, fast asleep, and the other two

were using it as a cushion, resting their

elbows on it, and talking over its head.

There are bridges on the rivers,

As pretty as you please;

But the bow that bridges heaven,

Next came the guests,

mostly Kings and Queens,

and among them Alice

recognized the White Rabbit.

Alice's Adventures in Wonderland, Chapter 8

Next came the guests, mostly Kings
and Queens, and among them Alice
recognized the White Rabbit.

Cross that bridge when you come to it.

These words were followed by

a very long silence, broken only

by an occasional exclamation of

"Hjckrrh!" from the Gryphon

and the constant, heavy

sobbing of the Mock Turtle.

Alice's Adventures in Wonderland, Chapter 9

Lesson 75 Exercise

These words were followed by

a very long silence, broken only

by an occasional exclamation of

"Hjckrrh!" from the Gryphon.

"Come on!" cried the Gryphon,

and, taking Alice by the hand,

it hurried off without waiting

for the end of the song.

Alice's Adventures in Wonderland, Chapter 10

Lesson 76 Exercise

"Come on!" cried the Gryphon,

and, taking Alice by the hand,

it hurried off without waiting

for the end of the song.

The Rainbow

And overtops the trees,

And builds a road from earth to sky,

Is prettier far than these.

"Oh, a song, please, if the Mock Turtle would be so kind," Alice replied so eagerly that the Gryphon said, in a rather offended tone, "Hm! No accounting for tastes!"

Alice's Adventures in Wonderland, Chapter 11

"Oh, a song, please, if the Mock

Turtle would be so kind." Alice replied

so eagerly that the Gryphon said,

"Hm! No accounting for tastes!"

Whatever is worth doing at

all is worth doing well.

Narration: Belling the Cat

The Caterpillar
by Christina G. Rossetti

Brown and furry
Caterpillar in a hurry,
Take your walk
To the shady leaf, or stalk,
Or what not,
Which may be the chosen spot.

No toad spy you,
Hovering bird of prey pass by you;
Spin and die,
To live again a butterfly.

"There, now I think you're

tidy enough!" she added as she

smoothed his hair and set him

upon the table near the Queen.

"There, now I think you're

tidy enough!" she added as she

smoothed his hair and set him

upon the table near the Queen.

Brown and furry

Caterpillar in a hurry,

Take your walk

"O Tiger-lily," said Alice,
addressing herself to one
that was waving gracefully
about in the wind. "I
wish you could talk!"

"O Tiger-lily," said Alice,

addressing herself to one that

was waving gracefully about in the

wind. "I wish you could talk!"

Laughter is the best medicine.

After this, Alice was
silent for a minute or two.

pondering. The Gnat amused

itself meanwhile by humming

round and round her head.

After this, Alice was silent for

a minute or two, pondering. The

Gnat amused itself meanwhile by

humming round and round her head.

"I was thinking," Alice said

very politely, "which is the

best way out of this wood.

It's getting so dark. Would

you tell me, please?"

"I was thinking," Alice said very

politely, "which is the best way

out of this wood. It's getting so

dark. Would you tell me, please?"

To the shady leaf, or stalk,

Or what not,

Which may be the chosen spot.

The boat glided gently on, sometimes among beds of weeds and sometimes under trees, but always with the same tall riverbanks frowning over their heads.

Through the Looking-Glass and What Alice Found There, Chapter 5

The boat glided gently on, sometimes

among beds of weeds and sometimes

under trees, but always with the same

tall riverbanks frowning over their heads.

A good name is rather to be

chosen than great riches.

Narration: The Bundle of Sticks

Alice could not help her lips

curling up into a smile as

she began. "Do you know, I

always thought Unicorns were

fabulous monsters, too! I

never saw one alive before!"

"Do you know, I always thought
Unicorns were fabulous monsters,
too! I never saw one alive before!"

No toad spy you,

Hovering bird of prey pass by you;

Spin and die,

To live again a butterfly.

"I always do," said the Red

Knight, and they began

banging away at each other

with such fury that Alice

got behind a tree to be out

of the way of the blows.

"I always do," said the Red Knight, and

they began banging away at each other

with such fury that Alice got behind a

tree to be out of the way of the blows.

Make hay while the sun shines.

"Do you know why they're so
fond of fishes all about here?"

"Do you know why they're so fond
of fishes all about here?"

do   due   know   no

they're   their   there

so   sew   here   hear

Dusk in June
By Sara Teasdale

Evening, and all the birds
In a chorus of shimmering sound
Are easing their hearts of joy
For miles around.

The air is blue and sweet,
The few first stars are white,
Oh let me like the birds
Sing before night.

And she caught it up and
gave it one little kiss.

And she caught it up and

gave it one little kiss.

Evening, and all the birds

In a chorus of shimmering sound

Are easing their hearts of joy

For miles around.

It is a very inconvenient

habit of kittens (Alice had

once made the remark)

that, whatever you say to

them, they always purr.

It is a very inconvenient habit

of kittens (Alice had once made

the remark) that, whatever you

say to them, they always purr.

Do unto others as you would

have others do unto you.

Narration: The Lion and the Mouse

Narration: The Lion and the Mouse

They had each of them a
hundred enormous snakes
growing on their heads, all
alive, twisting, wriggling,
curling, and thrusting out
their venomous tongues!

They had each of them a hundred

enormous snakes growing on their heads,

all alive, twisting, wriggling, curling, and

thrusting out their venomous tongues!

Dusk in June

The air is blue and sweet,

The few first stars are white,

Oh let me like the birds

Sing before night.

Dusk in June

Perseus left the palace, but
was scarcely out of hearing
before Polydectes burst into
a laugh, being greatly amused,
wicked king that he was.

Perseus left the palace, but

was scarcely out of hearing

before Polydectes burst into

a laugh, being greatly amused,

wicked king that he was.

An old fox is not easily snared.

"Behold it, then!" cried
Perseus, in a voice like
the blast of a trumpet.

"Behold it, then!" cried Perseus, in a
voice like the blast of a trumpet.

The stranger's smile

grew so very broad that

it seemed to fill the room

like an outburst of the sun,

gleaming into a shadowy dell.

A Wonder-Book for Girls and Boys: *The Golden Touch*

The stranger's smile grew so very

broad that it seemed to fill the

room like an outburst of the sun,

gleaming into a shadowy dell.

A Bird Came Down the Walk
By Emily Dickinson

A bird came down the walk:
He did not know I saw;
He bit an angle-worm in halves
And ate the fellow, raw.

And then he drank a dew
From a convenient grass,
And then hopped sidewise to the wall
To let a beetle pass.

He glanced with rapid eyes
That hurried all abroad,—
They looked like frightened beads, I thought;
He stirred his velvet head

Like one in danger; cautious,
I offered him a crumb,
And he unrolled his feathers
And rowed him softer home

Than oars divide the ocean,
Too silver for a seam,
Or butterflies, off banks of noon,
Leap, splashless, as they swim.

A Bird Came Down the Walk

A bird came down the walk:

He did not know I saw;

A Bird Came Down the Walk

He bit an angle—worm in halves

And ate the fellow, raw.

If he loved anything better,

or half so well, it was

the one little maiden who

played so merrily around

her father's footstool.

If he loved anything better, or

half so well, it was the one little

maiden who played so merrily

around her father's footstool.

Haste makes waste.

Narration: The Shepherd Boy and the Wolf

"How provoking!" exclaimed

Pandora, pouting her lip.

"I wish the great ugly box

were out of the way!"

"How provoking!" exclaimed Pandora, pouting her lip. "I wish the great ugly box were out of the way!"

A Bird Came Down the Walk

And then he drank a dew

From a convenient grass,

A Bird Came Down the Walk

And then hopped sidewise to the wall

To let a beetle pass.

If you were left alone with

the box, might you not feel

a little tempted to lift

the lid? But you would not

do it. Oh, fie! No, no!

If you were left alone with the
box, might you not feel a little
tempted to lift the lid? But you
would not do it. Oh, fie! No, no!

One man's trash is another

man's treasure.

Here and there, peeping

forth from behind the

carved foliage, Pandora once

or twice fancied that she

saw a face not so lovely.

Here and there, peeping forth

from behind the carved foliage,

Pandora once or twice fancied that

she saw a face not so lovely.

"That's no more than fair,

and I'll do it!" quoth the giant.

"For just five minutes, then,

I'll take back the sky."

"That's no more than fair, and I'll do it!" quoth the giant. "For just five minutes, then, I'll take back the sky."

He glanced with rapid eyes

That hurried all abroad,—

They looked like frightened beads,

I thought;

He stirred his velvet head

is not   are not   was not

he is   she is   it is

had not   could not   will not

he will   she will   they will

O my sweet little people, you

have no idea what a weight

there was in that same blue

sky, which looks so soft and

aerial above our heads!

O my sweet little people, you have

no idea what a weight there was in

that same blue sky, which looks so

soft and aerial above our heads!

Write it on your heart that every

day is the best day of the year.

Narration: The Arab and His Camel

Their food was seldom anything

but bread, milk,

and vegetables, and now

and then a bunch of grapes

that had ripened against

the cottage wall.

Their food was seldom anything but

bread, milk, and vegetables, and now

and then a bunch of grapes that had

ripened against the cottage wall.

Like one in danger, cautious,

I offered him a crumb,

A Bird Came Down the Walk

And he unrolled his feathers

And rowed him softer home

The milk pitcher, I must not
forget to say, retained its
marvelous quality of being
never empty when it was
desirable to have it full.

The milk pitcher, I must not forget
to say, retained its marvelous
quality of being never empty when
it was desirable to have it full.

One good turn deserves another.

"My good wife Baucis has gone to see what you can have for supper. We are poor folks; but you shall be welcome to whatever we have in the cupboard."

"My good wife Baucis has gone to see

what you can have for supper. We are

poor folks; but you shall be welcome to

whatever we have in the cupboard."

He was as wild, as swift, and
as buoyant in his flight through
the air as any eagle that
ever soared into the clouds.

A Wonder-Book for Girls and Boys: *The Chimæra*

He was as wild, as swift, and as buoyant

in his flight through the air as any eagle

that ever soared into the clouds.

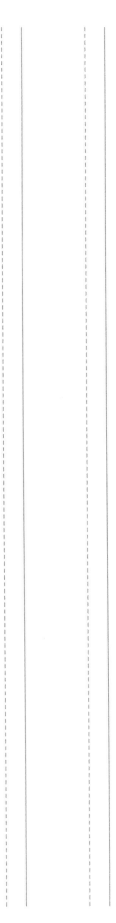

Than oars divide the ocean,

Too silver for a seam,

Or butterflies, off banks of noon,

Leap, splashless, as they swim.

"And one other time, as I was coming to the fountain with my pitcher, I heard a neigh."

"And one other time, as I was
coming to the fountain with my
pitcher, I heard a neigh."

It's not over till it's over.

Narration: The Town Mouse and the Country Mouse

Narration: The Town Mouse and the Country Mouse

Made in the USA
Columbia, SC
14 August 2021